Tea Light
Moments
FOR A
Woman's
Soul

Hope Lyda

HARVEST HOUSE PUBLISHERS

EUGENE, OREGON

Cover by Garborg Design Works, Savage, Minnesota

Cover photo © Garborg Design Works

TEA LIGHT MOMENTS FOR A WOMAN'S SOUL
Copyright © 2009 by Hope Lyda
Published by Harvest House Publishers
Eugene, Oregon 97402
www.harvesthousepublishers.com

ISBN 978-0-7369-2407-8

Printed in the United States of America

10 11 12 13 14 15 16 / BP-NI / 10 9 8 7 6 5 4 3 2

Acknowledgments

~

Gratitude flows when I think of all the wonderful people who have prayed me through the past couple of years. When you run out of words to lift up on your own behalf, you finally learn how to rest in the prayers of others. So thank you to all women who take time to pray for the needs and lives of others and specifically to those who have covered me. There are too many to name here, which is a lovely, humbling thing.

Thanks to my mom, Jean, and my sister, Dawn, for their support and love. And to my mother-in-law, Julia, who has recently faced several years of trying times with strength and grace.

A heartfelt thank-you goes to the entire editorial team at Harvest House. Not only are they a talented bunch, but they are prayerful, compassionate, and generous.

Special thanks to my editor, Peggy Wright, who radiates compassion and has this incredible ongoing conversation with God. She does not just have a prayer life…she lives a life that is a prayer.

And to you, the reader…thank you for joining me on this path of exploration, hope, and belief. We make the journey as individuals, but we learn of the journey from one another.

Contents

God of Light

So now I can walk in your presence,
O God, in your life-giving light.

PSALM 56:13

When my friend Jackie and I had the good fortune to travel through France and Italy, we visited many famous cathedrals as well as chapels too small to be listed in the tour books. I purchased crosses and postcards. I took pictures of murals depicting the life of Christ. I put a penny in a machine to have Abe Lincoln's visage stretched and replaced with a pressed image of Notre Dame. But the greatest souvenir that I brought home was the ritual of lighting a candle and saying a prayer. When I entered these sanctuaries, I lit tea lights nestled in ruby and amber glass holders and then sat in worn pews, resting in the silence. Surrounded by the hope of prayers whispered throughout centuries to the God of light, my spirit was renewed.

This souvenir, carried home in my heart rather than my backpack, reminded me how vital and transforming it is to express my life to God and wait upon the Divine. I am guided by his light, his truth…but first I must seek him.

There is something soul-warming about lighting a

candle and staring momentarily at the flame as it builds and subsides. My hope is that you will feel a sense of fulfillment and comfort as you read through these meditations. My prayer is that you will experience a time of connection with God as you light a candle or pause during your day with these devotions and prayers.

Take a deep breath. Watch for your own souvenirs of the sacred.

Hope Lyda

I need to take an emotional breath, step back, and remind myself who's actually in charge of my life.

JUDITH M. KNOWLTON

Sweet Offerings

Whatever scent of candle you choose to light, make your time of meditation and prayer a sweet offering to God.

- Light a lavender candle for relaxation.
- Light a chamomile candle for peacefulness.
- Light a peppermint candle for refreshment and invigoration.
- Light spice candles like cinnamon and clove for motivation.
- Light a citrus, mint, or bergamot candle for energy.
- Light berry candles like cranberry, mulberry, or strawberry for refreshment.
- Light a eucalyptus candle for revitalization.
- Light a rose candle for reflection.
- Light a sandalwood candle for stress relief.
- Light a vanilla candle for hospitality.
- Light a ginger candle for a mental boost.
- Light an unscented candle for radiance and calm.

They also brought spices and olive oil for the light, the anointing oil, and the fragrant incense. So the people of Israel—every man and woman who was eager to help in the work the LORD had given them through Moses— brought their gifts and gave them freely to the LORD.

EXODUS 35:28-29

Light a Candle
for Awareness

A Moment to Breathe

I make the most of all that comes
and the least of all that goes.

SARA TEASDALE

I need just a moment. To catch my breath. To take in wonder. To explore my thoughts. To consider my faith. To reflect on the day. To wait and listen. When I look at my schedule and consider how many moments come and go, wasted on mindless tasks or rote thoughts, it is no surprise that I feel worn out and have very little to show for it. Moments of silence allow us to listen for the cues and leadings that the whir of our autopilot feature tends to drown out.

What currently keeps you from silence? Is it the busyness of your day, the rhythm of your life, the pulse of your own expectations? Maybe the better question is: Which came first, the avoidance of silence or the busyness? I believe our ability to sit with the silence and in silence depends greatly on what we experienced during our childhood. Chaos breeds chaos, and calmness breeds calmness. However, if we experienced an extreme of either of those, we might crave the other out of a desire to protect or comfort ourselves. While some of us are just more naturally inclined to crave solitude, I believe that we are all created to experience those moments of silence and of seeking. This is when we can feel and know God's presence.

Still moments before God allow us to welcome what the day has to offer. We are less likely to cling to the burdens of yesterday or clench our fingers around today in anticipation of tomorrow's possible concerns. Honor this day. Celebrate its unfolding as you celebrate your own awakening.

Shedding Light:

- Consider what keeps you from practicing moments of silence. Prepare a place or a time that allows for a bit of refuge.
- What does the clamor of your routine sound like—traffic in motion, coworkers in conference, cries of little ones, the ring of a cell phone? Wait for these sounds to settle. The voice of God is beneath them.

Prayer:

God, grant me a heart, mind, and spirit that are open to all that today offers. Help me make the most of what comes my way and make the least of what goes.

Afterglow:

Today I will be awake so that I can see and feel all that God reveals.

Sit with Me

*Then Jesus said, "Come to me, all of you who are weary
and carry heavy burdens, and I will give you rest."*

MATTHEW 11:28

Stepping into God's presence is not always easy for me. It is never a question of his whereabouts, but of the location of my thoughts. When I'm ready to be quiet, still before God, my thoughts often are of me...and my list of transgressions mostly. That ever-stinging regret turns a chance for reflection into either a pity party or a guilt trip. So I'm either surrounded by my liveliest, most drastic mishaps, or I'm packing up my baggage and mentally distancing myself. Neither scenario ushers me into silence, focus, or to God's side. I *feel* that I can't enter God's presence with these blatant flaws from my past and the ones fresh from this morning. It seems a bit like joining the queen of England for tea while wearing my favorite sweats—the ones with holes in the knees and the hem threads draping like fringe. It's not proper. Pious. Or very polite.

Well, here's a big difference: Chances are that the queen isn't inviting you or me to tea. But *God is* inviting us to spend time with him. In the blink of a spiritual background check, he knows about those flaws and that entire year or period in your life when you ignored him. And yet the invitation arrives anyway. "Join me," it says. And best of all, it closes with the perfect line, "Come as you are."

Shedding Light:

- What do you believe you have to achieve, do, or be before you can sit with God? Clear away those human expectations of worthiness and replace them with thoughts of God's invitation to come to him with all your burdens, flaws, and needs.

- If God calls you to him, no matter your state of imperfection, are you willing to drop everything and savor such acceptance?

Prayer:

God, I come with baggage, as you know. I'll work on giving that over to you, piece by piece. Forgive me for holding back because of my feelings of unworthiness. They keep me from baring my soul. They keep me from your presence.

Afterglow:

I'll stop making excuses so that I can be real before God and experience the wonder of grace.

It's Getting Crowded

If one does not know to which port one
is sailing, no wind is favourable.

SENECA

Did I turn off the oven? Are my tags about to expire? Will our tree fall over with the next big wind? Let's see, if the mortgage check went through before the electrical check, I might be in trouble. Did I drink the last of the milk? I wonder how long road construction can possibly last! The price of stamps went up again... These are my thoughts in the span of a split second. Whether I'm driving to a meeting or standing in line at the grocery store or walking down the hall after a late evening trek to the bathroom, these thoughts storm through the sorely ineffective barricades in my mind and take over my conscious and subconscious life. They leave me unfocused, frazzled, and longing for direction.

It's getting too crowded in here...in my mind and heart. I'm filled and overflowing, but not with the reflections my life and spirit crave. I want to spend moments fully aware of mercy's tenderness, of God's leading, of gratitude's buoyancy. But it takes concerted effort to quiet the crowd of daily surface details and musings to get to the depths of God-thoughts. This is our chance to do just that...to make the effort toward intimacy with God. There are so many concerns and ideas worth contemplation. Wait for the crowd to die down and clear some space to explore purpose, redemption, and the joy of being alive in this moment.

If you never allow time to ponder your direction, your heart, and those deeper thoughts that rumble below the chatter of the mind, you will not be in tune with your life or the direction God is leading you.

Shedding Light:

- Identify and list which reoccurring thoughts keep you up at night or interfere with your concentration during the day. Spend a few moments praying over these specific concerns.

- Was there ever a time in your life when you more readily explored questions of God, faith, and wonder? What can you do now to recapture that spiritual level of contemplation?

Prayer:

Lead me to your feet, Lord. I want to sit and listen as you speak truth into my life. Keep me from crowding out those times when a song of praise rises up in my spirit or a prayer drifts from my heart to my tongue. These times will honor you.

Afterglow:

I'll allow my thoughts and prayers to go deeper. I'll spend time considering more than the worldly concerns that usually occupy my mind.

The Flame of Faith

There are two ways of spreading light: to be
the candle or the mirror that reflects it.

EDITH WHARTON

Fire and water. These powerful elements and their attributes often star in prose—from poetry to liturgy. They are used metaphorically and literally to provide us with deeper understanding of our spiritual and physical lives. Many of us have stepped forward to be immersed in water…to be baptized. To demonstrate and complete the giving of ourselves over to God, we rise up out of the swelling river, the splashing baptistery, or a lake dotted with swaying boats at summer camp—and we are a new spiritual creature, buoyed by hope and dripping in grace. We become a part of God's light, a refraction and reflection of his shining countenance.

Because of the water, we carry the flame of faith. The ignited torch of belief lights the way for us in times of shadows and cascades brilliant sparks, like a Fourth of July display, when we celebrate life's immeasurable wonder. God is our source of light. And a life cast in reverence, joy, compassion, and belief becomes a mirror to reflect that light within our circumstances, our families, our circles—no matter how big or how small—and our world.

The ebb and flow of water is much like the rise and wane of a fire. Both can carry us toward deeper belief.

Shedding Light:

- What has carried you toward belief in the past and what does so today?
- Does your flame of faith burn brightly, or does it need renewal?
- Try to find ways in your everyday living to become a mirror held up to holiness.

Prayer:

The elements of fire and water are nothing compared to the power of your love that illuminates this life before me. Remind me to tend to the flame of my faith so that it never subsides. May it never cast light upon my own doings but always reflect your goodness.

Afterglow:

Today I light a candle. It's a simple act, but it renews my faith.

New View

Acknowledge and take to heart this day that the LORD
is God in heaven above and on the earth below.

DEUTERONOMY 4:39-40 NIV

From my perch on the penthouse level balcony of a rented urban condo, I saw a city with new perspective. It wasn't my city, but it was a city I have enjoyed numerous times by walking the steep streets for hours, observing the locals and tourists, and savoring cuisine served up at every corner. But I'd never noticed how impressively far the bay stretches beyond the celebrated shoreline market. I'd never looked up at the many birds staring down from telephone wires. And I'd never witnessed how many people crisscross intersections simultaneously seven blocks apart.

We maneuver through our days, make choices, and pursue purpose with a street-level view of living. God's eye view presents a scene much more vast and eternal. Yes, God is there with us when we walk the pavement or have our nose to the grindstone, but God also sees how failure and forgiveness intersect up ahead in our journey. He knows that the small stumbling block we dismiss today will turn into a bigger trial down the road. And when the obstacle in front of us seems insurmountable, he sees how small it is in light of his power.

He is the Lord in heaven above and on the earth below. We live here, but our mind-set and perspective can be that of heaven, if we take time to look up now and then.

Shedding Light:

- Look at life differently by depending on God's vision.
- Give whatever seems overpowering or unmanageable over to God's purpose and plan, so that he can put the situation into right perspective.

Prayer:

My view is so limited. I want to trust you with every turn, every step. Guide me today and lead my human heart in the ways of heaven above. Help me understand that even when I cannot see beyond today, you see and know my future.

Afterglow:

I'll look up more often…not just to take in a greater view but to call upon the One who sees all.

What Springs Up

*Inside myself is a place where I live all alone, and
that's where I renew my springs that never dry up.*

PEARL BUCK

Awareness isn't only about seeing and doing what is in
front of us. Awareness is also about seeing what we ignore. Spiritual awareness leads us to uncover the intangibles
that seek our time and affection. Those mental distractions
we shoo away may be the exact thing we are meant to pay
attention to. If we are sitting at a table with our bills splayed
out and our checkbook open and our mind wanders to
how we'd like to go on a mission trip to Brazil, a dream has
just attempted to capture our attention. Dreams, goals, life
questions, and prayers emerge when we least expect them.

The multitasking nature many of us have adopted has
its benefits, but what falls by the wayside are those brief
encounters of understanding that surface and require more
thought and consideration. We are too busy cleaning our
email inbox, sending a fax, and answering our phone, so
the spiritual leading gets squelched. Trading efficiency for
spiritual deficiency is not a good trade.

Practicing awareness ultimately requires us to pay attention to these hopes and musings when they spring up. They
don't come to us as whispers because they are unimportant,

they emerge as whispers because they deserve our undivided, rapt, lean-on-the-edge-of-our-chairs attention.

Shedding Light:

- Spend less time shooing away dreams and more time musing over them.

- When was the last time you listened to your dreams? Where did they lead?

- Can you think of an idea that you squelch on a regular basis? Give it space.

Prayer:

I want to be centered and not scattered. Teach me the wisdom of silence. When my spirit resists it and I fill my time with activities and my ears with voices, music, media, and dialogue…lead me to the quiet whispers of my soul and of your will.

Afterglow:

When I pay attention, I am more connected to my life and to God. I will listen for my heart to speak up today and will be prepared to take notes.

Light a Candle
for Delight

Spice It Up

*Don't be afraid your life will end: be
afraid that it will never begin.*

GRACE HANSEN

Habanera, cayenne, cumin, chipotle, clove, jalapeno, cinnamon, and chile piquin. This could be the beginnings of a deadly burrito sauce, but because I'll never be someone who appears on the Food Network, this, instead, is a recipe for joy. Spice, zip, and zest might not make their way into many meditation books, but when it is time to talk about delight, we must turn to our senses. What better way to ignite them than with something that has a bit of fire? I bought a hot chocolate mix with Mexican seasonings a couple weeks ago, and it was fabulous. I instantly had a new passion (and respect) for hot chocolate, the drink formerly known as a poor substitute for good coffee.

What infuses your soul with a wonderful burst of heat and flavor? Is it a quick dive into a clear, blue pool? A splash of red on your fingernails? The idea of a Saturday road trip with no particular destination? A book, a beach, and a bottomless iced tea? The exhilaration of running along a river trail? The smile of your spouse or the tender kisses of your children? It might be something that initially scares you—like making a new friend or starting a new career.

Embrace whatever adds spice to your spirit and faith. It might transform what once seemed like a poor substitute for a good life into...a good life!

Shedding Light:

- Tap into whatever motivates and excites you about life—such things can be directing you to your intended passion and purpose.
- If delight seems to be something that only others experience, create your own recipe to spice up your life. Start with a challenge or a time of prayer asking for awareness.

Prayer:

My bland existence is a meager offering to you, God. I want to live with vibrancy and spark. Rekindle in me the passion for living that ushers your children to a life of amazing delight.

Afterglow:

I'll add seasonings and spices to my life. Out of gratitude, I'll seek to live each day with passion and wonder.

Joie de Vivre

Take delight in the LORD,
and he will give you your heart's desires.

PSALM 37:4

Does it seem decadent to delve into the topics of desire and passion? Have a few misguided romance novels or cable channels caused us to eliminate such words from our language—even when we are talking about our spiritual journey? What an unfortunate loss! Our spiritual journeys are absolutely, undeniably, unapologetically supposed to be filled with desire and passion. And yet many of us temper our emotions, even when they swell with gratitude for all that God is and does in our lives. We walk away from hardship experienced by strangers—and sometimes even friends—because their intense need reminds us of our frailty and deep longings for acceptance and love. Instead of embracing miracles, we reduce grand, life-changing God-moments to the size of coincidence by rationalizing them with human reason or attributing them to human responsibility.

Joie de vivre, the joy of living, is not a dirty phrase, nor is it reserved for the French, though we could learn a lot from their pursuit of simple pleasures. Don't put out the fires that stir your heart and lead you to impassioned and emboldened faith. Desire leads you to find the One who can fulfill your every longing. Passion leads you to gratefully serve the One who seeks to give you the delight of your heart and soul.

Shedding Light:

- What ignites your passion for living, serving, and being?
- Make the connection between your gifting and your desires. How might the gifts God has given you lead you to fulfill the desires of your heart?

Prayer:

What a gift this life is! God, I want to make the most of this life you have given to me. Let my passions be yours for me. Show me how to use my gifts—to reveal and use them for godly, fulfilling purposes.

Afterglow:

I will work "desire" and "passion" back into my spiritual vocabulary.

Unguarded

When we were children, we used to think that
when we were grown-up we would no longer
be vulnerable. But to grow up is to accept
vulnerability...To be alive is to be vulnerable.

MADELEINE L'ENGLE, *WALKING ON WATER*

Do you take joy in the smallest of things? Or have you become a bit cynical...always prepared to brace yourself for the worst-case scenario or for someone else's sarcasm? Many of us have become guarded. Cautious. Doubting. Serious. What if we met each new day with an anticipation of joy? Instead of becoming uptight by the quirks and shortcomings of others, find a way to be amused by them. Not with a twinge of condescension, but with the happiness of grace. A renewed, vulnerable spirit can emerge from behind the walls we've put up to keep us from harm or disappointment.

When does your guard go up? With certain family members? At work? With strangers who trigger your impatience? Revisit these people or these circumstances with a refreshed spirit of joy. Let a bit of levity brighten your mood, mind-set, and manner. This becomes an act of good will and good nature that ultimately reflects God's love. Amusement will override annoyance. Wonder will outweigh worry. Self-protection will open up to compassion. And through the act of becoming vulnerable and lighthearted, you'll discover a deeper sensitivity to God's leading, wisdom, and will. You'll discover what delights await the heart that welcomes and accepts.

Shedding Light:

- When do you shut yourself off or distance yourself emotionally? Try countering these situations by changing your attitude in advance.

- Lighten up whenever possible. Add more fun and laughter to your life starting this week.

Prayer:

Lord, you created laughter and joy. You don't want me to wallow in complaints, insecurities, or conflict. These become my barriers to spiritual growth and delight.

Afterglow:

I will release judgment of myself and others, so that I can share God's love more readily and more willingly.

Skipping and Clapping

Some pursue happiness, others create it.

AUTHOR UNKNOWN

Go to any playground, and you'll find a wisdom that surpasses any book-learning you've had. It is the understanding of unadulterated joy. Children aren't taught the ways of joy. It bubbles up from their soul and expresses itself in their broad, welcoming grins and their wide-eyed expressions of awe—both are usually followed by unaffected laughter.

What I really like to see is the way children physically throw themselves into life's delight. They don't politely smirk or chuckle. They display physical comedy like they've been training as comedians, but it's even better because it's pure in intention—they're expressing their heart's joy. They clap their hands in celebration of sunshine, flowers, bugs, or bath bubbles. They smack their lips after tasting something delicious. They hum to music—even when there is no music to be heard. They slap their hand on their short thighs like a cowboy after a good campfire joke. And they skip! They half-run, half-dance across a lawn on a Saturday afternoon or down the hallway at school to greet a friend.

Couldn't we get back to that purity somehow? Can we

remember our first sips of delight? How sweet. How rich. How fulfilling. And, oh, how we wanted to share it!

Shedding Light:

- Allow your joy to be shared physically—clap your hands in praise of someone's success or effort, give hugs, smile at your barista and mean it, and, if the situation presents itself, go for the skip. I'm pretty sure that even if you don't break out into pure laughter, someone will.

- Throw yourself into something that isn't about gaining success but about gaining joy and a thirst for life.

Prayer:

I've tasted pure joy, but it was a long time ago. When I equate life with routine, rules, and rigidity, remind me how to play and how to be a child of God—savoring delight without shame, self-consciousness, or judgment.

Afterglow:

I'll try a little physical comedy today. I'll express my joy or my affection without holding back.

Happy with the Present

Happiness is not a state to arrive at,
but a manner of traveling.

MARGARET LEE RUNBECK

There is great relief to be had when we stop dictating what will give us happiness and allow God to gently, or sometimes swiftly, move us toward true contentment. There are probably as many definitions of happiness as there are people, but many of us define joy in terms of something we hope *will happen* in the future. "I would be so happy, if I got that job." "Life would be so wonderful, if I didn't have so much responsibility right now." "Once I retire the good life will begin!" "When my kids get older, I'll be able to figure out what I want my life to be."

It is fine to hope for change or for things to be different, but if these future versions of life become our only example of joy…we'll never find the happiness that God has placed all around us in our immediate circumstances. Like buried treasures they lay hidden in the people, conversations, decisions, and possibilities we encounter daily but don't recognize. "What ifs" will, over time, undermine the great "what is" of your life. If you are hard-pressed to find blessings and delight in your current circumstances, don't pray for God to fast-forward you to a new scenario—pray for God to reveal those hidden treasures as you move forward in life.

Shedding Light:

- Stop waiting for happiness to come to you. Discover it in your present life.

- Consider how you've defined happiness over the years. Was that standard handed down to you by parents or by media or by career standards? Be sure you aren't borrowing someone else's version of delight, while you miss your daily opportunities to experience deep joy and satisfaction.

Prayer:

God, why have I adopted such an unattainable version of happiness as my standard? I want to stop selling my life short…I want to know the depths of happiness. Help me to become a person who creates joy and who invites others to join in.

Afterglow:

I will base my happiness on the security of God's love and his desire for me to know the fullness of joy.

Treasure Hunt

Don't store up treasures here on earth.

MATTHEW 6:19

Consider what you hold dear. Such things are your true treasures. While you might have your eye on a particular car or dream about adding a hot tub to the backyard and a walk-in closet to your bedroom, these are only small delights compared to those that are less of the world and more of God. Whatever your day holds, imagine that you are on a treasure hunt of the heart. Gather what sparkles with beauty and shines with goodness.

When you encounter people, look beyond their clothes and past their initial greeting. Try to see them as a whole. What about their character is admirable and wise? Is their heart kind and generous? If you have children, think on their most wonderful traits. Before you ask your children, yet again, to do the dishes or finish their homework, be sure to tell them about the gems of delight you see in them. Invite your entire family to search for godly riches daily.

Your treasure hunt will lead you to a wealthier appreciation for life and its abundance. It will also inspire you to notice more about today and worry less about tomorrow. When you are busy gathering heavenly treasures everywhere you turn, worry cannot dominate your outlook. In fact you'll start seeing even the difficult situations in a new light.

Shedding Light:

- Look for the good in others. Make it your mission to recognize strengths and abilities in anyone you meet.

- What would you hope others recognize in you as a treasure?

- Are there some earthly treasures you hold onto that get in the way of your ability to appreciate and gather godly riches?

Prayer:

I want to be someone who is attracted to the good in people and in the world. I can become pretty fixated on what is falling apart or lowly gossip or the troubles that might come tomorrow. These are not worth attention or time. Remind me to pursue and acquire true treasures.

Afterglow:

Today I will look for the silver linings of situations and people.

Light a Candle
for Prayer

Craving God

Prayer is as natural as breathing, as necessary as oxygen.

EDITH SCHAEFFER

Have you had times when you craved communication with God? This should be our natural state of being! If and when we try to live separately from his breath, nourishment, and power, our existence is a mere shadow of the experience we are intended to have as God's creations.

Prayer is our direct connection to God's heart. Without prayer we walk through our days with a concept of God but without communion. We hold God up as deity but do not embrace him as Father. Your need for intimacy with God is as natural as your need for oxygen. Through our relationship with our Creator, we are refreshed, revived, and renewed.

Your need for the source and the source that fulfills your need do not change. Each day you require that connection all over again. Day in. Day out. When you weep privately over brokenness and pain and know that only God's presence will bring healing, you are seeking that connection. When you feel small in the world and call out for direction and meaning, you are seeking that connection. When you feel a craving deep in your spirit and an overwhelming need for God is pressed upon your heart, you have found the source for living. Breathe it in.

Shedding Light:

- Do you seek connection with God only after you've exhausted everyone else on your cell phone contact list? Try him first next time.

- Brokenness and gladness alike lead us to God, if we are paying attention.

- What leads you to God? Loneliness, sadness, joy, decisions, conflict, transition? Consider these as gifts if they redirect your heart to prayer and communion with God.

Prayer:

You're right there. Right here. And I still overlook the power of communion, connection, and covenant with you, God. Help me keep my focus upon you, so that my heart seeks you first in every situation.

Afterglow:

I'll stop filling my need for God with everything and everyone else *but* God.

Aware of Prayer

*Devote yourselves to prayer with an
alert mind and a thankful heart.*

COLOSSIANS 4:2-3

With great kindness we quickly offer to pray for others. It is second nature to receive an amazing blessing and think *God is good.* When our hearts are filled with compassion, we want nothing more than healing and hope for ourselves or another. It's not always our habit to follow these up with actual prayer. And why is that? I'll speak of the elephant in the room (someone has to point it out)…prayer doesn't always seem like a real action.

When our prayer life feels shallow, we're probably tossing out prayers halfheartedly. When our prayer life feels one-sided, we're probably not waiting to hear God's part of the conversation. God may be catching a glimpse of our heartfelt needs or our gratefulness, but we're missing out on genuine dialogue. Welcome opportunities to pray for others and your own life. Be grateful for anything that leads you to God's feet. Enter a time of prayer with an alert mind and an alert spirit…ready and waiting to receive God's compassion, love, and healing.

As you light a candle, as you carve out a still, calm moment in the day's perpetual activity, recognize your need for God in and through everything you face. Resting in the very real strength of unconditional love is the most important thing you can do today.

Shedding Light:

- If prayer feels less than real, figure out what element is missing. Are you truthful when you speak to God? Are you vulnerable? Are you even talking to God or are you talking *at* God?
- Prayer doesn't require perfection, but it does require participation. Make the effort.
- Alertness doesn't come easy. Give yourself rest, nutrition, exercise, and silence and see if you are more awake for your times of prayer (and more in tune with your life).

Prayer:

I will sit with you today, God, because I know that you see me, hear me, and know me. I'll sit with you because there is peace in your presence. I'll sit with you even when the right words don't come to me because I know you know my heart inside and out. I'll sit with you because it's time I recognize prayer as one of the most meaningful gifts you created.

Afterglow:

I will start treating the action of prayer with more respect. I will become faithful in this way.

Simplicity of Prayer

*You can pray while you work. Work doesn't stop
prayer, and prayer doesn't stop work. It requires only
that small raising of mind to Him. "I love You,
God, I trust You, I believe in You, I need You now."
Small things like that. They are wonderful prayers.*

MOTHER TERESA

Poignant prayers have been scribed over the ages. But such petitions don't soar to heaven more quickly or with greater priority than a simple prayer spoken in the middle of the day while you drive to work, clean a bathroom, or stir-fry vegetables. Well-crafted verses are fine to read when you want to be carried to a mood of meditation and praise, but they aren't necessary for either of those experiences to take place. How it must delight God to hear your musings, questions, and fast words of thanks as you go about your day. These heart-to-heart calls strengthen the bond between Creator and creation.

What are your most frequent prayers during a day? *Thank you. Take this from me. Help. Lead me. Forgive me. Heal me. Show me. Carry me.* You can discover a lot about how you relate to God by looking at how many heartfelt calls you make and of what nature they are. You'll also see where the voids are in your communication. If you tend to yell "help" and rarely offer up "thanks," start to expand your gratitude during the day. If you praise God and whistle as you work and yet rarely ask for leading, you might blissfully and blindly be traveling a path that is of your own making.

Make heart-to-heart calls a regular part of your day. Don't wait for an illuminated moment of extreme emotion or spiritual awareness. Lift up the small things as they are the foundation of our lives. They are the gifts you have to offer your God.

Shedding Light:

- What are your most frequently uttered prayers? Which kind of prayers do you tend to forget about? Try to mix it up. Experience depth in your dialogue with God.

- Pray without an agenda. See what God places on your heart when you stop dictating the conversation's direction. It helps if you take time to breathe deeply and wait upon God.

Prayer:

Forgive me for missing out on the wonders of prayer. I am so quick to offer up my needs that I forget to inquire about the needs of others. Or I forget to lean upon your wisdom and ask for direction as I take small and big steps forward. May I also learn to hold my tongue, so that I can feel your hold on my heart.

Afterglow:

When my head takes over my time of prayer, I will stop and let my heart speak.

Lift It Up

Accept my prayer as incense offered to you,
and my upraised hands as an evening offering.

PSALM 141:2

I know it can seem strange to have the ear of God. To be able to speak whatever is on your mind and heart openly and with emotion. There are parts of me that I would rather hide from God because they are embarrassing, humiliating, and cast me in a not-so-favorable light. But there is even more reason to expose them...so that God can give me a discerning heart that knows the difference between my ignorance and his wisdom.

Don't be afraid to be honest with the One who knows you so very well. He has seen your flawed, regrettable moments of acting human and self-centered, but he has also witnessed the victorious moments when you trusted in him. Your prayers—those authentic, difficult, and revealing prayers—are an offering made to God. You go before him naked and dependent, and he clothes you with compassion and mercy. Times of confession make our times of praise that much more poignant because we know that God's love is genuine and his grace is vast. Being humble before the Lord is a part of prayer. Kneeling down and bowing one's head is not an image that belongs only on a Sunday school poster. That image should reflect the state of our hearts as we lift up our offerings of prayer.

Shedding Light:

- False humility is an obstacle to a deeper prayer life. Get real with God. What parts of your life do you hold back from sharing?

- When have you kneeled before the Lord? Try making it part of your daily prayer time. Bowing down is not merely theatrics…it is an action that leads you to a place of submission, vulnerability, and humility.

Prayer:

God, sometimes I pick and choose what I bring before you in prayer. I want every aspect of my life to be under your authority and in your care, and yet I hold back. Sometimes because of fear and intimidation and sometimes because I'm lazy. I come to you today with my worries, failures, and even my shallowness fully exposed. Fill me. Teach me. I pray to be made whole.

Afterglow:

I will bow down physically, spiritually, and emotionally to show my reverence for the One who hears me and loves me unconditionally.

Light a Candle
for Hope

It's Plantin' Season

There is more hope in a fresh future. A new season has begun, one in which I will let some fields lie fallow while others will be prepared for planting.

Joan Anderson, *The Second Journey*

God will give you the seeds and the desire for the harvest of hope to come, but you'll need to do the planting. What is the condition of the soil of your life? Are you hardened? Are you spiritually dry and longing for refreshment and renewal? Have the weeds of apathy, complacency, or guilt taken root where your hopes are meant to be firmly planted? Find ways to tend to your garden. Have moments of meditation, spend time in prayer, reflect on God's Word, and watch for God's goodness to take root.

If you've experienced circumstances that have drained your life's soil of its most vital nutrient—faith—then spend time feeding your soul. Read inspirational writings of those who have faced trials or droughts and who now speak of a harvest of grace and belief. Pray your questions and ask your questions of those who know you and have wisdom. Break out of your routine, so that the oxygen of new life breathes in and out of your days.

Once your heart and soul are prepared to receive God's hope for your life, you can begin sowing those precious seeds of discipline, belief, faithfulness, and trust. Soon you will see the bright green stems rise up out of the soil and the colorful blossoms open up in full bloom. Gather them into a bouquet. And when a bloom is about to fade, there is another season of growth awaiting you in the garden. Gather another bouquet just as remarkable as the first. This is the bounty of hope. Keep planting and wait upon God for the harvest of hope fulfilled.

Shedding Light:

- If there is anything keeping you from cultivating hope, try to weed it out of your life. Clear a space to plant the seeds God gives to you.
- Hope is not in limited supply. If the hope of your youth has faded, seek the new colorful harvest God intends for you to have during this time.

Prayer:

I don't necessarily feel despair, and yet my life seems low on hope. Even though I send up prayers with faith, I don't always plant the discipline, belief, faithfulness, and trust that you give to me. Help me be a more diligent gardener, so that the harvest of my life reflects your bounty.

Afterglow:

I won't treat hope like a rare flower anymore. I'll pluck it up every chance I get and return for more.

Innocence

There is a divine plan of good at work in my life.
I will let go and let it unfold.

RUTH P. FREEDMAN

When the world encounters innocence, it wants to call it naïve and out of touch. The world wants to tear it down by listing evidence of disappointment and pain. Innocence looks cheery, red-cheeked, optimistic, and shiny. Our tendency is to be skeptical of such a pure presentation.

Maybe at one time you were that fresh face of innocence. Was your heart so full of hope and possibility that you couldn't wait to spread the news of such wonder? Did doubt or hardship cause you to hold back your hope just a little and then a lot? It can happen to even the most faithful believers. In fact it can more easily happen to the most faithful believers because they are the ones who are putting themselves out there with a fragile heart full of hope.

Life isn't always fair or right or righteous, but this doesn't mean that we should dismiss innocence as a sweet but misguided quality. Innocence sees the good in circumstances and doesn't give up searching for that act of kindness or that ounce of compassion in a stranger's face. Innocence might get smudged along the way, but its shiny hopefulness is never diminished because its light burns from within and is fueled by the God of hope, the God of peace, and the God of grace.

Shedding Light:

- Are you the one who has an innocent, pure sense of life, or are you the one who convinces others that they need to toughen up or "get real"?
- Give your wounds to God. Allow innocence back into your life.

Prayer:

God, help me to spot innocence and try to preserve it. Don't let me give up on people or on the chance to encounter goodness and wholeness. My heart has been broken, but you have moved me beyond that point of hurt. Give me the courage to return to full living by hoping for the best and seeing the best in others and in the fresh face of each new day.

Afterglow:

I will be less of a naysayer and will say more in support of innocence, purity, grace, and kindness.

Hope for the Modern World

In spite of everything I still believe that people are really good at heart. I simply can't build up my hopes on a foundation consisting of confusion, misery and death.

ANNE FRANK

As I walk by a contemporary sculpture on my way down a city street, the afternoon sun causes the creation to shimmer. It is of three whimsical figures pieced together with metal of various shapes. Each figure has its own special characteristics, but they all have something in common— their "arms" are spread wide open. When I look back at the structure from a lower point along the hill, it reminds me of Calvary, and I find myself drawn to its simple power. Regardless of the artist's intention, I am moved by the idea of a modern Calvary.

I think of how intertwined my life is with Christ's suffering on Calvary and how this advent in the Christian faith is ultimately one of hope and resurrection, not death and destruction. We are creatures pieced together by the Artisan's hand. We are called to be shining crosses that radiate with wonder and who, with arms outstretched to friends and strangers alike, become three dimensional reminders of the Calvary message our modern culture so desperately needs. Some people might walk on by. Some may never take notice. Others might dismiss you as a strange interpretation. But others will be drawn to the simple power, and their lives will forever be changed by eternal hope.

Shedding Light:

- Have you made faith so complex that you have missed the simple power and beauty of the cross?
- Do you take time to see yourself as the Artist sees you?
- How can your life reflect hope and resurrection? What would that look like?

Prayer:

Creator, your hands formed me, and you placed me here in this time and place and circumstance. Open up my heart to care deeply for everyone who comes into my life, whether for the long term or for a fleeting moment.

Afterglow:

I will open my arms and heart wide to bring the message of Calvary to others.

Intentional Waiting

If we could for a moment see the cosmic implications
of our waiting with and for God, we would be
astonished at the glory of "ordinary" things in
our lives, and the significance of other people.

ISABEL ANDERS, *AWAITING THE CHILD*

If we were in control, we would collect all those minutes "lost" while stopped at traffic lights, on hold on the phone, and waiting in lines and deposit them back into our life account. But thankfully that isn't an option. If we pay attention, these occasions of worldly waiting are a training ground for spiritual waiting. Maybe there is no differentiating between the two. All forms of waiting become a spiritual practice because they require us to recognize that we are not in control—one of the hardest lessons we'll ever face.

But when we wait with and for God, there are even more important lessons to embrace. We discover that there is beauty in our wounds. We learn to accept gracious help from others rather than pride ourselves in our independence. During our wait for physical healing, we learn more about our need for spiritual healing. As we long for transformation, God grants us a vision of hope to carry us and those around us. When waiting feels less than divine, we have the opportunity to see how complete reliance on

God is an extraordinary gift. And when we long for God's leading but end up waiting and wondering if it is all in vain, the One who is in control makes a deposit of faith in our life accounts.

Shedding Light:

- See waiting as an opportunity to grow spiritually.
- How has independence kept you from full reliance on God?
- What are you waiting upon God for right now? Pray specifically for this during your waiting moments throughout the week.

Prayer:

I have allowed my distorted sense of priority to dictate how I view waiting. I get frustrated when I am asked to slow down or to hold back from rushing forth with my plan and agenda. God, pace me. Show me the rhythm of life that leads to greater understanding of you. Teach me the spiritual blessing of waiting.

Afterglow:

I'll spend time deliberately looking for the glory in the ordinary.

Hope Recycled

May all who fear you find in me a cause for joy,
for I have put my hope in your word.

PSALM 119:74

How do you get hope? Do you receive encouragement from the comments of others, the support of family, the network of friends you have created? When you face trials, are you drawing on the strength and sustenance from God's Word? Are there ways you commune with God that offer renewal and restoration?

You are fortunate to have faith and hope. Many people have not yet discovered their way to renewal and the promise of grace. The great thing about hope is that it is a reusable and renewable resource. Quite a rarity for something that is such a hot commodity. But if you don't draw from your reserves and offer it to others, you are halting the cycle that God intended for the things of hope. Consider how many people you encounter each day who are eager for any remnant of peace they can hold in their hearts. What good does it do anyone if you provide an example of a life lived in hope and yet you do not share the source?

Think of how you first found hope. Who passed it on and took time to share it? Who was willing to recycle the gift of security, possibility, and faithfulness when you needed it most? Watch for opportunities to do the same for anyone God brings into your life. Reduce your inhibitions and open up about your faith. Reuse the encouragement you've experienced. And recycle the hope of God's limitless love.

Shedding Light:

- When have you withheld hope? When have you passed it along?
- Is it an inner-conflict, a deeply rooted fear, or a strong stubbornness that keeps you from freely sharing hope, hopefulness, and the peace of faith? Ask yourself why you do hold back.

Prayer:

You've seen me do it before. I've started to reach out, and then in an instant, I pull back the offering of hope I was about to make. Sometimes my insecurities about faith prevent me from sharing who you are. I want to rest in your love and ignore the fears and doubts that challenge my desire to connect. Better yet I want to replace those fears and doubts with peace and never hesitate to share the endless gift of hope.

Afterglow:

I'll question why I hold back from reaching out today. I won't let that become my nature.

The Science of Hope

*Hope begins in the dark, the stubborn hope
that if you just show up and try to do the
right thing, the dawn will come. You wait
and watch and work: you don't give up.*

ANNE LAMOTT

In junior high science class, a friend and I decided to do our own experiment in addition to the assigned one. We were working with seeds and petri dishes. The specifics escape memory. But what I do recall was entering the science room each day and heading straight to the formerly unused drawer, discreetly opening it up, and checking on our sprouting seedling. I think it struck us as funny to have this private experiment actually growing and probably doing better than the one we would be graded on, but there was also the thrill of creating something out of nothing. Or so we thought. We, of course, started with a seed—a seed that was already designed to grow. We were not practicing deep science as much as we were recording the journey of hope.

It turns out that our hope in Christ is a lot like that experiment. There are times when we are in the dark. We experience bouts of grief, disconnection, depression, sorrow, loss, or doubt, and the light we once walked in seems to fade with each passing day. Maybe you are going through such a season right now. Take heart. When we carry God's hope, it is with us in the dark. It is never dormant. It waits beside us and slowly grows, day by day, even in the absence of visible light. There is nothing that can separate us from the science of hope—it is already designed to grow within us.

Shedding Light:

- Has darkness covered you this year? What evidence of hope has taken root in that darkness?

- You might be called upon to help a friend or even a stranger wait in the darkness. Are you prepared to sit with them and be part of the hope that is rising in their life?

Prayer:

I'm designed to grow in your love and strength. God, have mercy on me in these times of darkness. I fumble along, striving to see shapes that are familiar and signs of what might lie ahead. I forget to look within…at the seeds already planted in me. You work such wonders in my life. When I feel like quitting, help me remember that I'm designed to be one of your miracles.

Afterglow:

When night covers my life, I'll put fear aside and watch for the dawn.

Light a Candle
for Compassion

Upon a Star

I believe in prayer. It's the best way we
have to draw strength from heaven.

JOSEPHINE BAKER

Stars guided shepherds in the time of Christ. Stars still orient sailors and hikers and help fishermen make their way through the night. Their usefulness is commendable. But it is their other role that makes me a fan. When they wink and glitter against the dark sky, they invite us to speak our hearts. Did you ever close your eyes and wish upon a star for a pink-frosted birthday cake or a chance to meet your favorite singer? The expression of even small hopes is a tender act of faith.

Prayers of adulthood are more wonderful than wishes of childhood because we know who hears these pleas, requests, and expressions of happiness. And we know that our wishes don't rise a mere 500 feet in the air and dissipate into the atmosphere. They soar with clarity all the way to the ear of God, and he gladly hears them—silly, serious, deep, or simple.

In the middle of a very hard year, I lifted up prayers for simple things like open parking places, sunshine, and afternoons of solitude. God knew that I had more important things to pray about because he was the One covering me through the difficulties. But as these lighter wishes left my lips, I doubt he was concerned about my shift toward shallow. I believe he had compassion for the woman with her eyes closed and her heart open who was asking for help to make her way through the day.

Shedding Light:

- Keep your connection with your Creator throughout the day by allowing your heart to speak freely and frequently.
- What is your adult equivalent of a pink-frosted birthday cake? Make a wish, say a prayer.
- Receive God's compassion in your life. Your small and big concerns matter deeply to him. He awaits those late night, whispered prayers.

Prayer:

My prayers as a young girl were true and pure. I've lost that a bit along the way. I've probably tried to impress you with my theology. Such a loss it is to stop speaking of my heart's big and small desires and hopes. God, I want to be that young girl again in spirit. I want to look to you with big eyes and an open heart and share about my day.

Afterglow:

I'll allow the childlike, simple wishes to lead me to deeper faith.

Humble Pie

Always be humble and gentle. Be patient with each other,
making allowance for each other's faults because of your love.

EPHESIANS 4:2

Apple pie is extra tasty with a dollop of ice cream.
But humble pie is made to be served with a side of
compassion. Why do humility and compassion go together
so well? Have you ever eaten "humble pie"? Have you ever
had to go to another person or to a group and admit to a
mistake, a sin, a failing, and accept the consequences? It is
an uneasy, painful, and revealing process.

Your heart is never the same after being humble before
others. Some people become hardened and angry because
wounds are exposed when pride is stripped away; these are
the people who mistakenly ordered their humble pie with a
side of revenge. They think the act of humility destroys their
dignity when, in fact, humility served with compassion
restores dignity after ego, judgment, or greed undermines it.
The heart becomes softer when one's eyes are opened up to
the purpose for compassion. Human compassion welcomes
others into its embrace even as we struggle to accept ourselves
as fallible. God's compassion covers us when we deserve to
wallow in our man-made pit of despair.

God will accept your meager words and your broken

thinking and mend you from the inside out. There is no room for spite when a heart is filled with grace and understanding. Those who have tasted compassion, when they deserved nothing but punishment or ridicule, become the people who forever serve the Lord with passion and who bestow compassion on others readily.

Shedding Light:

- Seek God's help to shed pride, so that you can know the humility of a servant's heart.

- When are you most full of pride and boasting? Is it when you are at work, with family, among friends, or when you are among strangers and feeling insecure?

- Approach your pride-triggered situations with a heart of compassion. Put God's love in the space between you and other people, so that there is no room for your insecurities.

Prayer:

I humble myself before you, God. I am proud and stubborn and independent. I've even ignored the needs of others because I've been focused either on my abilities or my inabilities so much that I don't recognize the opportunities for compassion and grace. Show me how to extend grace to others and to myself.

Afterglow:

I will stop protecting myself from the responsibility of asking for forgiveness or acting with humility, so that I can know grace.

Dog Shopping

Change really becomes a necessity
when we try not to do it.

ANNE WILSON SCHAEF

For years I've ignored my husband's comments about how our yard is *perfect* for a dog. And when he gets the cats to act like canines by training them to do tricks before they are allowed out the back door, I just smile and pretend that's normal.

I prefer to cohabitate with cats. We have one sweet one and one neurotic one, and that suits me fine. We can pile food in the dish, refresh the water, tidy the box, and say "See you when we get back, girls" as we head out for a weekend. A dog would be a lot of work and would require so much more attention and planning.

There are many logical reasons not to get a dog, but I want to let go of self-protection philosophies and tactics that keep me from embracing change. I want to believe that good things come not only when I simplify life but when I am willing to expand it. I want to be compassionate enough to make choices that include the visions and hopes of others. For example, the cats will appreciate being cats rather than stand-ins for dogs. And my husband will have the joy of a wish fulfilled.

When we finally find "the one" and the volunteer at the shelter looks at me and my sweater laced with cat hair, I plan to go the way of hope and kindness and boldly say:

"I want a dog. Please."

Shedding Light:

- What don't you want to do? Is it because you fear change? Is it because you don't want to give in? Release your hold and see what might unfold.

- Sometimes standing firm in our ways and in our opinions and beliefs is just an overly righteous way to remain frozen, unable to grow or trust.

Prayer:

Okay, so I'm holding onto something for the wrong reasons. You've seen me this way before…when I've said no to your calling because I was too intent to follow my preferred path or place in life. I don't want to miss out on the adventure of trusting you with what comes next. Let my life open up to the unknown.

Afterglow:

I'll risk failure or mistakes if it means I have a chance at the abundant life of faith.

Pre-Ramble

A loving silence often has far more power to heal
and to connect than the most well-intentioned words.

RACHEL NAOMI REMEN

Words get in the way of communicating compassion. We get in the way of communicating God's heart for others. Have you ever tried to express your sorrow, only to have a friend interrupt and introduce her struggle and sadness? I've done it to others, and I've had it done to me. I think it is a natural response. It probably comes from a desire to connect with the other person's need. That's the forgiving viewpoint. After all, what says "I understand" better than explaining our own encounter with a similar problem, plight, or loss? And doesn't it say we understand *more* than others if we also talk about our cousin's journey through the same thing, how we were by her side, even when it cost us time and energy that we'll never get back?

Nope.

Compassion doesn't have to be communicated along with your bio, resume, family tree, or pain credentials. Others don't always need hard proof that you can empathize. They need gentle proof, the kind that comes with nods, hugs, and prayers. There are times when your testimony will give great relief and comfort to another person. But before you begin to speak, take time to listen. Listen to a wounded friend's words and body language. Don't rush the person toward a resolution for their situation because there might not be one…not today. And don't force your own tidy answers onto another's difficult circumstance, or you'll stifle their willingness to share their doubts and deepest needs.

Most importantly, when they struggle to find the right words, stand with them in silence. When it feels uncomfortable, that is the beginning of true empathy. Often it is in the silence that a heart awakens to God's healing.

Shedding Light:

- How uncomfortable are you with the silence of another? Is it your pain or your friend's pain that you rush to cover with words?

- Consider several ways to show compassion to another that do not involve words, but only actions, thoughts, or prayers.

Prayer:

When I am the person in need of the healing silence of compassion and friendship, I first seek you and your presence. You offer a balm that eases my deepest worry, my sharpest pain. I look for this care from others and sometimes it is there, sometimes it cannot be found. Give me a discerning heart when I am around anyone who weeps or who longs to weep.

Afterglow:

I'll learn the languages of sorrow and of comfort and become proficient at listening to both.

Mighty Mercy

To love deeply in one direction makes
us more loving in all others.

ANNE-SOPHIE SWETCHINE

I watched the tide come in with awe. A bazillion drops of water form a wall that swells, climbs, rolls, and then pushes in one direction toward the shore. It is futile to try and stand against one of these big waves; it will carry you in its intended destination.

Farther down the beach, there are high sand plateaus and lower pits, the water does not come as a unified wall. It pools and swirls. There are small waves within larger waves and they grab at random sections of the shore. There is force, a powerful undertow churns, but there is no unity.

God's mercy is a mighty wave in our lives. And when we love in that one direction, in the direction God's mercy and love is flowing, we too become part of that powerful wave. If our love is scattered, random, and only doled out to a select few, our love becomes a conflicted, unpredictable force like the undertow. I challenge you to love God wholly and completely. Give yourself over to his mighty mercy. It is powerful enough to carry you to its intended destination—love.

Shedding Light:

- What do you love so strongly that you get caught up in the power and direction of that love?

- Have you been caught in the undertow, unable to choose a direction or reach the shore of a goal or a dream?

- Have you let love wash over you? Allow yourself to feel God's love that fully today.

Prayer:

When I try to stand against the wave of mercy, it isn't long before I feel the power of your love working through the situation. I am called to fall back into your strength and follow the way to love. Thank you for carrying me. For leading me with strength and compassion, so that I can experience your grace, not only personally, but as it extends to those around me.

Afterglow:

I will give myself over to loving deeply, no matter the risk, no matter the fear, no matter the doubt…I will follow the way of God's mercy.

Birds of a Feather

*Two people are better off than one, for they
can help each other succeed. If one person
falls, the other can reach out and help.*

ECCLESIASTES 4:9-10

As the change of season brought sunnier weather, my friend enjoyed the opportunity to sit outside and be entertained by the sweet birds that emerged simultaneously with the colorful new blossoms that bordered the yard. The feathered, lively tourists congregated daily around her pond and drank, ate, and bathed with contentment. After several days my friend noticed that these birds had a built-in system of support and protection. One bird always stood "guard" while its peers took care of life's necessities.

In our lives we face many changes of season. Whether the change is brought on by age, loss, transition, or opportunity, we rely on the flock to help us along. Maybe someone drives you to the doctor's office, a neighbor watches the kids on short notice, or a friend delivers dinner when life is just plain overwhelming. The family we are born into as well as the one we create present a way for us to experience God's support and protection. We all need friends who stand with us or for us and who have our back while we take care of life's necessities. And we all need to be that friend when one of our own faces their challenge of change—big or small.

Shedding Light:

- What season are you facing? What seasons are your friends and family members facing?
- Do you entrust your times of hardship or change to your "flock"?
- Do you entrust your seasons to God?

Prayer:

Give me the strength I need to make it through this transition. I have hope for tomorrow even as I struggle with today. You have blessed me with friends and family who seek the best for me. I pray that I am willing to share my burdens with this support network…and may I come to you with my every need.

Afterglow:

I'll accept help today. And I will humbly accept the prayers and support of those you bring into my life.

*Light a Candle
for Creativity*

Dawdle

*So you see, imagination needs moodling—long,
inefficient, happy idling, dawdling and puttering.*

BRENDA UELAND

I used to be an expert dawdler. As a kid I loved to get lost in music and books—they transported and filled me. I'm sure there are arguments against cultivating a mind that so readily goes to the interior, but it was the beginning of my quest for creativity and invention.

Sadly the world of adulthood has shifted me toward productivity, deadlines, tasks, and a preference for getting things done. This way of life doesn't nourish my soul. I've lost the ability to quickly and gladly settle into a vacation day or a book. Worries override my ability to imagine my day differently. I want to see my life with fresh eyes and a creative mind each morning.

Learn to dawdle with me. Whether you were ever good at it or not, we should give it a try. Sitting in silence can work. Lighting a candle is a start. Gazing at the moon for 15 minutes after the rest of the household is asleep is fabulous. Heading to your backyard with a glass of lemonade and a book is right on track. Lying in a hammock while your mind drifts to how you'd like to grow your garden next year is perfect. When you catch yourself trying to rush by a slower person at the grocery store or along the river path, hold back. Breathe in. Walk to match their pace. They might be an expert dawdler, and you could learn a lot.

Shedding Light:

- Have you been able to dawdle as an adult? Were you able to as a child?

- What frees you? Is it a palate of vibrant colors? An afternoon of no responsibility? A warm, lazy summer's day? A blank page in a sketch book? Discover what sparks your sense of creativity and frees your spirit.

- What keeps you from savoring life? Spend time exploring the obstacles, so that you can overcome them and fill your life with more whimsy and wonder.

Prayer:

God, help me to still my spirit. Guide me toward the deeper waters of stillness and reflection. Show me how to make the most of an afternoon by "wasting" it with nothing planned. May I use the gift of dawdling to praise you, serve you, and discover more about life's riches.

Afterglow:

Even if I have to schedule it…I will take time for dreaming, napping, staring at flowers, drawing scribbles, skipping stones, or whatever strikes my fancy.

Watching for Your Cue

No matter what happens, keep on beginning and failing. Each time you fail, start all over again, and you will grow stronger until you find that you have accomplished a purpose—not the one you began with perhaps, but one you will be glad to remember.

ANNE SULLIVAN

The curtain opens and reveals a stage full of musicians sitting with backs straight and bows and hands poised above instruments. The musicians don't scan the audience, they intently watch the conductor and await their cue to begin the music. And when it begins, it fills the concert hall with the sounds of grace and light.

When we struggle to live an inspired, creative life, it might be because we are looking to the crowd for approval or permission. Instead of allowing ourselves to do what we love, we take a survey of our closest friends (and critics) or of the pop culture to see if our pursuits have merit.

I can tell you—without taking the survey—that those longings have great worth and validity. Go ahead and draw, even if your last picture was of a neon green cow and a purple, oblong moon. Feel free to write, especially if your eighth-grade English teacher said you lacked imagination. If you were known as the neighborhood klutz, take a few spins about the living room. Decorate your bedroom in a color that nurtures you even if it is off-trend. This is living a life of explored beauty.

And when you get stuck in judgment, sit at attention and keep your eyes on the Conductor to await your cue. He'll direct you to create something of grace and light that could only come from your inspired soul.

Shedding Light:

- When have you sought permission before exploring an area of interest or passion? How did that turn out?

- Which activities connect you to a sense of God's delight? Create the opportunity for these activities and make them a greater part of your life.

- Become familiar with beauty by seeking it in others and in yourself.

Prayer:

God, help me embrace joy. I let today's worries overcome me. I let the questions about tomorrow override my happiness. Lead me to the creative part of me that I've stifled with to-do lists, expectations, and regulations. Help me find the passions you have planted in the deepest part of my soul.

Afterglow:

I'll take my cues from God. I won't take my cues from critics and complainers.

Language of the Soul

Dance is the hidden language of the soul.

MARTHA GRAHAM

Today's a day to get out and move. Become aware of your body and how it connects you to your mind, heart, hopes, and to God. That sounds like an overstatement of benefits, but it isn't. If we consider movement only physical in nature then we miss out on much joy and wisdom—the very aspects that could inspire you to move more often. Martha Graham said that dance is the language of the soul. She wasn't a theologian, she was a dancer. And she experienced the heart's ability to express itself when a person uses rhythm instead of reason and leaps instead of logic.

Moving loosens up the body and then dislodges those stubborn bits of anger, worry, frustration, or grief that can build when we leave them to sit like stones in the stomach. Many women use their time of walking as a time to pray. It's a perfect combination. While our limbs, muscles, and bones join together to send us in a particular direction, our spirits can seek direction from God.

As an observer and introvert, I like to sit and reflect. But when I force myself out for a walk, I find that the creative juices start flowing. Ideas, connections, theories, prayers, and answers bubble up to the surface. It's as if the mind and spirit join in as soon as the feet start moving. Step on out there and see what comes to mind and spirit when you show God gratitude for your intricate, miraculous body by using it.

Shedding Light:

- Find a way to move and a time to move that allows you to spend time processing, creating, and praying.
- Avoid the inclination to mask your thoughts with music or television while you are moving. Take the creative jaunt outside and stay tuned in to what comes up from within and what you experience during your encounter with your chosen environment.

Prayer:

Speak to me, God. I want to feel your voice inside of me. I want to stop rushing around and start moving intentionally. Give strength to my body and soul as I make adjustments in my life. I want more creativity in my life. I want to be open to your leading. May my thoughts turn to you as soon as I step outside and walk forward with hope and without an agenda.

Afterglow:

Today I will breathe in and out while moving my body and loosening up the inner areas of my heart, mind, and soul.

Powered by Optimism

No pessimist ever discovered the secret of the stars or sailed an uncharted land, or opened a new doorway for the human spirit.

HELEN KELLER

If God says "go," do you take a step back, so that you can weigh the pros and cons? And do you come up with a whole lot more cons each round? Even people who have the strength of hope and faith find themselves restricted by their limited attitudes. Along the way many of us learn to fear new things and avoid uncharted territory.

Pessimism causes us to see a very narrow slice of what life is and can be. Chances are that God is directing you beyond that narrow slice...and beyond your comfort zone. What good is it to say that you are someone who relies on the love and guidance of God in one breath and then say "no" to every opportunity to actually rely on the love and guidance of God?

When life is going well, we don't want to rock the boat. And when life is a bit rocky, that's when we say, "See, life is hard and unpredictable. I should stick with what is safe right now." This is not a life lived in God's power. This is a life fueled by fear. Commit today to living a life powered by optimism and hope. Reject the voices of the past or even the resumé that shows you have stumbled. After all, those have no power anymore. In you God has created a new life. Live it.

Shedding Light:

- When have you made choices fueled by fear? Fueled by faith? How are these experiences different?

- List your biggest fears. Face them so that they do not sneak up on you. Don't dwell on them but pray for the spiritual antidote to that fear. For example if your fear is that you will never be loved, pray to feel the presence of God's love in new ways. If you fear that something bad might happen to you, pray for protection but also pray for a deeper reliance on God—the kind that will carry you when circumstances are difficult.

Prayer:

My fears blur together. I hardly know what I am specifically afraid of anymore. I feel uneasy and often worry. God, pull me out of this way of thinking and living. I want to rest in your peace and your will. Confidence gained through faith will lead me to a much more authentic life than one controlled by concern. I trust you. I lean on you.

Afterglow:

I'll step out of my comfort zone today to see how big life is beyond my limited scope.

Courageous Creativity

Each of us has an inner dream that we can unfold
if we will just have the courage to admit what
it is. And the faith to trust our own admission.
The admitting is often very difficult.

JULIA CAMERON

Is there a dream that God has given to you that makes you smile when you think of it? What keeps you on this side of fulfilling it? It becomes easy to stifle a dream by holding it too close. Share it and it has the space to grow. If the dream doesn't seem complete in your mind's eye, you're probably right. Most great ideas present the initial impetus for something bigger. The missing pieces will come into view once you put that dream out into the world. You might have half of an idea and someone you meet in three months might have the other half. Or something you are going to learn in the near future might give your dream more dimension and direction. The lesson God gives you today might be in preparation for the fulfillment of this dream.

Do you have gifts and talents that you'd like to use more often? Do you feel the tug to step into a leadership role with a ministry or an organization that touches your heart? Have you walked by a house in your neighborhood numerous times and wished that you had the guts to introduce yourself to the woman who lives there? Your dream might be as simple as finding a friend or as involved as starting a business. Small or big…dreams begin with the courage to recognize what God is building in your heart. They unfold when we confess them as a possibility!

Shedding Light:

- Make a mental list of your hopes. Choose one or two and then reveal your "secret" to a mentor, a group of girlfriends, or to your spouse.

- See how the people you encounter and the things you learn today could relate to the dream that God has placed on your heart. Be attentive to the unfolding!

Prayer:

Help me see how you are working in my life and the lives of others. I will give you praise for this journey I am on because I am dependent upon you and your strength. I won't ever know what tomorrow holds, but I will know that you are here with me, you see the big picture, and you have known of me and my life before I even existed. I can't wait to see how the dreams you give to me become experiences that lead me closer to your heart.

Afterglow:

Today I will watch as you shape my dreams and bring new ones before me.

Start a Trend of Truth

*When a woman tells the truth, she is creating
the possibility for more truth around her.*

ADRIENNE RICH

You are a creator. You are an artist forming her life's work under the instruction of the Master. What you put out into the world is your creation. When you work hard to establish a comfortable, caring atmosphere in your home, you are creating a sanctuary. If you raise children to love others and to celebrate God, you are inspiring faith. When you speak kindness and peace into the lives of people who face pain and turmoil, you're inventing a life of compassion.

What you do today can set the trend for those around you. I love the fruit of the Spirit from Galatians 5:22-23. Let's look at them afresh as the materials God gives you, so that you can create a life's work that is honorable and holy. Love allows you to honor all of God's children. Joy celebrates life, and peace leads you back to God's presence. Patience waits for God's leading. Kindness reaches out without discrimination. Goodness inspires greatness in others, and faithfulness does not waver in the face of fear or insecurity. Gentleness eases the soul, and self-control reflects discipline and commitment.

Create a life that draws out your best and stirs a heart of faith in others. Create a breathtaking portrait of the Master.

Shedding Light:

- What are you creating? What have you created?
- Return your thoughts to the fruit of the Spirit daily. Find ways to express each of them through your actions, your intentions, and your efforts.
- Let go of behaviors that do not reflect the fruit of the Spirit. Pray them away. Pare them away.

Prayer:

I'm such an inconsistent role model. Help me become whole, balanced, consistent, and true in all that I do and say and profess. Where I am weak, help me glean strength through my trials and questions. Where I am false, help me dig deeper until I uncover the root of my insecurity and exchange it for your truth.

Afterglow:

I will find ways to create goodness. I will find ways to inspire truth.

Light a Candle
for Purpose

The Way of Light

Simplicity is an ongoing process, a joyful experience of detaching ourselves from what is less important and attaching ourselves to that which is more important.

BARBARA DEGROTE-SORENSEN, *'TIS A GIFT TO BE SIMPLE*

The evening before a company was coming to haul away our recyclables and junk, I gathered stuff from every corner of the house and created a pile in the living room. With growing enthusiasm I scoured rooms, looking for more ways to lighten my load and create more space.

It's surprising how things that are initially functional can become a burden. That candy dish you bought at Cape Cod was a prize find—now it's hidden in a cupboard behind your broken alma mater coffee mug and a hen-shaped egg timer, and it's in the way of pans you *do use*. It's time for it to go.

A similar fate awaits many intangibles we acquire—habits, routines, or ruts. Behaviors that once were functional may now be a burden. Even dysfunction serves a function initially. We gather attitudes, defense mechanisms, or lies that help us feel safe or in control. But when we give control over to God, the purging needs to take place, and it needs to continue. Every day we can eagerly and gratefully round up our sins, imperfections, and broken pieces and toss them onto a pile. And every day God is there to haul away our useless stuff, replacing it with peace, light, a pure heart, and plenty of room for future good stuff. All it takes is a willingness to simplify this life you lead, so that you have room for the life God calls you to lead.

Shedding Light:

- How do you burden your life with stuff? With busyness? With noise? What choices can you make to lighten your life today?

- Which habits from a life before faith still crowd your life today? How can you let go of them?

- Do you hold onto your sins and failings as tightly as you hold onto stuff? Release emotional burdens to God today.

Prayer:

My life has become cluttered and chaotic because I don't let go of those things that serve no purpose. Help me to recognize those actions or beliefs that actually prevent me from purpose. I want to give these over to you. I want to stop depending on temporal pleasures or pursuits and make space for a life of eternal importance.

Afterglow:

I will purge three things this week, and I will pray to release three unhealthy behaviors as well.

Anywhere But Here

*There is no need to go to India or anywhere else to find
peace. You will find that deep place of silence right
in your room, your garden or even your bathtub.*

ELISABETH KÜBLER-ROSS

*T*his can't possibly be where God wants me! Do you ever
think this? Do you look around and wonder how you
ended up "here"—a place in life and time that falls short of
your dreams or goals? Or maybe you've achieved your aspira-
tions, and they have not offered the fulfillment they promised
when they were far off in the distance, dangling like a carrot.

We can find disappointment anywhere...including where
we aren't. I wish that settling into our purpose was merely a
matter of gathering up our belongings, sending out change
of address cards, and carting furniture, a few books, and a
favorite lamp to another location. But that would be trying
to force a physical answer to address the spiritual question:
How can I find contentment and meaning in my current life
and circumstance?

First we need to stop looking "elsewhere" because that
leads us to deceive ourselves into believing that happiness
can *only* materialize somewhere else. It also causes us to
stop believing in God's amazing power to change our lives
and perspectives. Next we need to look to where there is

contentment and meaning—in God's peace and will. And last of all, take your discouragement or apathy—or whatever it is that first caused you to doubt—to God and watch him turn it into something useful for your journey of purpose: hope, understanding, discernment, grace, peace, anticipation, or wonder.

Shedding Light:

- Seek refuge in your own life for awhile. Give yourself the gift of time and nurturing.

- Light a candle, say a prayer, and step into rituals that breathe life back into your day and renew your sensitivity to God's gentle leading.

- What version of life do you pine for? Start investing in what is going on here and now. Things can and will change, but not if you stop working on your life as it is.

Prayer:

When my hopes became a long list of wants that left me feeling dissatisfied, they stopped being a part of my faith. They became excuses for me to complain. You have shown me that dreams can inspire my daily living in a healthy way when I give those dreams to you. Please give me a heart for the things you want to be a part of my life.

Afterglow:

I will see the wonder of my life right now. I will give each day to God as an offering and make the most of every moment.

Your Heart Will Follow

*Trust in what you love, continue to do it, and
it will take you where you need to go.*

NATALIE GOLDBERG

When our lives are directed by immediate needs rather than eternal hope, we will become stuck, thrown, lost, or flat out exhausted. And when that happens, all we want is a super long nap. Four days long would be ideal, but if you'll settle for a few cat naps and some times of prayer, I believe you'll be ready for this next step.

Start moving forward. You might not feel motivated or ready, but if you've become complacent or disheartened, you can get the momentum going. Have you experienced loss in your life? Reflect on that void, and then ask God to fill it up with his healing and renewal. If your job is dissatisfying or is consuming your energy, make time to do things you love—they could very well lead you to greater purpose. Is the weight of the world on your shoulders lately? Ease up on watching the news and take a break from filling your mind with images and sound bytes. Calm your spirit and pray without distraction—feel God's peace. If you lack motivation, yet desire to make a lasting change, seek accountability with others and commit to lifting up that area of your life in prayer daily.

It isn't always easy to break loose during those times of stagnation, but it is time to live life like never before. Your life matters, and this day in your life matters. Move forward today. A baby step or a big leap will send you on your way... and your heart will follow.

Shedding Light:

- Move forward—stop being stuck. Complacency or bitterness will set in if you don't give yourself over to God's momentum.

- Figure out what you need accountability for in your life, so that you can make lasting change. Set up a system of checks and balances either with friends or with goals.

- Breathe calm into your life little by little.

Prayer:

I'll follow you today, God. I'll make room for you. I'll stop rushing ahead with my expectations and demands because they only lead me to more frustration and life noise. Help me to listen for the still, small voice within. Where are you taking me today? That is what I will ask each morning. And then I and my heart will follow.

Afterglow:

I will show God the void in my heart, so that he can fill it with light and love.

What You Keep, What You Give

There is only one real deprivation, I decided this morning, and that is not to be able to give one's gifts to those one loves most.

MAY SARTON

We each have numerous gifts that we are born with, grow into, or are presented with during our faith journey. But the reason we have opportunity, inclination, or ability is not to raise ourselves up or to push forth our personal goals. Those gifts, often uncovered over time and during trials, are meant to be given to others on behalf of God. What might be a few of your gifts? Hospitality, service, leadership, musical ability, influence, sensitivity, creativity, teaching, praying, caregiving? The list of possibilities is as unique as you are. When you are not sure what gifts you have to give, start with the one we all have access to—a willing spirit. From that one gift, you can affect change, influence others, extend a helping hand, or raise the spirits and circumstances of those in need.

When gifts are saved and stored, they will form an ever-growing wall between you and your purpose. But when used and shared, our gifts lead us to a greater understanding of God's heart and his intention for our lives.

Shedding Light:

- Struggling to find your gifts? Ask others what they see in you. Take the risk of unraveling the mystery of who you are.

- Have you been storing up your talents…saving them for a moment of great success? Start using those in ways that grow the servant in you. You'll discover how multifaceted those talents are and how they grow exponentially when they are shared.

Prayer:

God, fill me with a sense of confidence and strength. When I try to hide behind my wall of insecurities, push me forward through the open gate of your will. When will I start trusting you with my life? All this time of faith, and yet I often move through my days like someone who doesn't know the mercy and might of the Creator. Show me those gifts and talents within me. Then show me how to start giving them away.

Afterglow:

I won't "save my best" for later or for any purpose outside of serving others and God.

Expect More

Don't live down to expectations. Go out
there and do something remarkable.

WENDY WASSERSTEIN

Responsibilities can be overwhelming, but let's face it…
there are many obligations and privileges that come
with being part of a family or the human race for that matter.
I have friends who are simultaneously managing the needs
of their children and those of their elderly parents. Some
things we sign on for—some are part of the life cycle.

Do you ever feel like you're living for someone else?
That you've taken on someone else's expectations for your
life? Expectations are different than responsibilities. When
expectations are shaping your motivation for the day, they
can turn your life inside out as you try to please someone
other than God and live a life that isn't true to your purpose
or calling.

If the expectations placed on you by others don't resonate
as true for you or your happiness, start declaring your own.
Life is way too short to have it dictated by guilt and guilt-
based decisions. I don't mean that you pack your bag and
head for the hills (you still have those responsibilities).
Instead search your heart, seek God's leading, and find the
direction that is your very own. Wouldn't it be great to live

for God as God intended? Go do something remarkable! What are you waiting for?

Shedding Light:

- If others have low expectations of you, step away from those limits and those deceptions.

- If you've bought into the need to maintain a high level of success, no matter the cost, then this is a destructive expectation that needs attention.

- Teach your children and others what life and living look like when grace replaces guilt.

Prayer:

Guilt. I know it is not of you, God. It never has been. I used to rely on conviction that did come from you…and that gently guided me in the right direction, toward big love and sweet mercy. But then I started listening to guilt and the expectations of others. I should've known that being bullied into righteousness was not your will. Reveal to me the leading of the Spirit and allow me to hear and follow your voice only.

Afterglow:

No more listening to guilt and expectations in stereo. I'll turn up the tune of grace and hum along.

You'll Be Filled

*Honor yourself, the truth of who you are. In so doing,
develop yourself fully mind, body, and spirit. Always
offer your service without measure. It will fill you up.*

BARBARA HARRIS, EDITOR-IN-CHIEF, *SHAPE* MAGAZINE

Inhale and exhale. Take a moment for peace and reflection.
There's plenty more busyness to come, so do this for
yourself freely. It is time to replenish that which seeps from
your being, bit by bit, during days filled with worry, fear,
second-guessing, performing, and juggling the impossible.
What do you need restored today? We can start with hope.
It is easy to lose it when we've been let down. God hasn't let
you down. Now for a little grace. No...make that a lot. This
has been with you all along, but you've forgotten to rest in
God's grace because you've been so strong and determined.

What else has been emptied from your soul? Truth.
Author Madeleine L'Engle wrote, "Truth is eternal, knowledge is changeable. It is disastrous to confuse them." As
knowledge shifts, stand on the secure ground of truth. It
will hold you. Peace always sounds so good. I think we believe it is intended for other people, those who don't live in
the chaos we do. *Maybe peace is for those who sit on moun-
taintops and chant,* we think. Say the word *peace* over and
over until it becomes a prayer and a reality. It is intended for

you. Love is in God's presence. We can turn love into an obligation, but God reminds us that it is a gift. If you don't "feel the love," extend love first. It is okay to give and keep giving as God directs. He will fill you with what you need.

Shedding Light:

- Have you mistaken changeable knowledge for permanent truth? Don't confuse the two. Grow in knowledge, and rest in truth.

- Is peace a stabilizing force in your life? Or is it still elusive. Study peace, sit with it, pray for it, and make it a daily practice. God's peace is yet another truth you can rest in.

Prayer:

Give me your peace. Show me whatever things or people I use as a source of comfort instead of your peace. Help me stand in your peace, so that it is my truth and my reality even as trials come and go, even in the face of questions about faith, and even when life is going along smoothly, and I'm tempted to take credit.

Afterglow:

I will spend time in meditation and be led to the peace of Christ.

Light a Candle for Transformation

A Little Praise

That is why I can never stop praising you;
I declare your glory all day long.

PSALM 71:8

A few words of praise can give us a sense of well-being, connection, and joy. A few words of praise can change our mood, shift our direction, and recreate our day. A few words of praise will transport us from the lowest depths to the highest heights. A few words of praise can remove the obstacles of hate and envy and free our way to love and compassion. A few words of praise lift the veil of human weakness and expose divine strength.

When words of praise are spoken, we are humbled and given insight into the might of God. Praise does more to brighten a life than any positive thinking or 15 seconds of fame ever could. Words of praise turn our slow walk into a happy gait. And when praise is given, we are reminded of the value and privilege of being a child of God.

When a few words of praise are spoken, we understand why there is nothing that we can't accomplish in God's power and will. All this goodness comes from a few words of praise...a few words of praise lifted up to our Creator.

Shedding Light:

- Do you spend time praising God during the day? If not, why is this absent from your faith life?

- Speaking praises honors God and reminds you that he is the source of all life.

- Once you start praising God, you'll find that you are better equipped to praise the people in your life freely because your identity and worth no longer depend on gaining credit in the world's eyes.

Prayer:

God, thank you for entering into a relationship with me. I'm just me, and you are the Founder and Creator of the world. How wonderful you are and how faithful. I have relied on your guiding hand to find my way. And when weary, I have fallen into your embrace time after time. I will praise you today for you are worthy.

Afterglow:

I will praise God this morning, this afternoon, and this evening. And tomorrow I will do it again.

Awaiting Transformation

What counts is whether we have been
transformed into a new creation. May God's
peace and mercy be upon all who live by this
principle; they are the new people of God.

GALATIANS 6:15-16

A restless spirit can cause us to question what we are doing and why we're doing it. Have you experienced that kind of inner agitation and not sure why? Restlessness can creep upon us when life is going along as planned. It can emerge when we're in between milestones and living life in a holding pattern. The restlessness can feel like crisis to some and like awakening to others.

When a hunger arises or uncertainties flood your normally steadfast thoughts, you might be inclined to doubt everything, but it is the perfect time to believe—to believe in what God is preparing in your heart and spirit. Those stirrings are possibly the birthing pains of wonder and growth. God is preparing you for a trial, a change, an epiphany, a ministry, or a deeper level of faith. Sit with the uneasiness and the anticipation. During this time of awareness pray for direction, thank God for the unknown, and prepare to experience life and faith differently. View the shift in your spirit as a gift, even if it is uncomfortable.

More unsure about life than ever before? Welcome to the beginning of your transformation.

Shedding Light:

- What triggers your uneasiness? What do you usually do to avoid exploring the root of it?
- Consider journaling through the uneasiness to see what is on the other side.
- Awakenings are not just for other people!

Prayer:

I feel as though my soul is pacing as it waits for something new, something meaningful to take shape. I've felt this before, but I've tried to ignore it by revving up my external activity. I don't want to be afraid of hunger and longing because they lead me to you. Direct me and my next steps.

Afterglow:

I will let hunger lead me back to God for answers.

Counseling Session One

*Why am I discouraged? Why is my heart
so sad? I will put my hope in God!*

PSALM 42:5

Sometimes what we need is an impromptu counseling session with no time to practice responses. Let's jump right into it and see what happens.

Imaginary Counselor: Tell me about it.

You: I made a big mistake, and I can't let go of it.

IC: You're human. Did you let go of it and give it to God?

You: Yes, but the guilt is strong, and I can't make it right. Why can't I fix this?

IC: God knows something that might help. I know it too. Ready?

You: Yes. But did I mention it was a big mistake?

IC: Here it is. You're human. Just as you need to know that God is bigger than your sin and he loves you unconditionally—you *also* have to recognize and admit that you are human. You can't fix this. God can.

You: I hurt others though. God must see that.

IC:	He sees that you're human. And he sees that you need him. That's how it works.
You:	I do need him.
IC:	And?
You:	My guilt won't make this right, only his grace does. I'm human and totally dependent on God to transform my sin into something resembling life and hope.
IC:	Now, we're getting somewhere.

Shedding Light:

- Speak to God directly, without practicing your responses. Discover what matters weigh heavy on your heart.

- How do you show God that you need him? Do others in your life see that you depend on God?

Prayer:

Forgive me for the times that I hurt others knowingly and unknowingly. When I am holding onto my life and my sin, help me release these to your power and grace. I want to live a transformed life. I pray to see my meek offerings turned into evidences of hope through your love.

Afterglow:

I'll accept that I'm human and express thanksgiving that God is the one who transforms my life.

Willing to Dream

Every great dream begins with a dreamer.
Always remember, you have within you the
strength, the patience, and the passion to
reach for the stars to change the world.

HARRIET TUBMAN

What do you want to change about your world? When your heart breaks because there is so much pain and suffering, have you forgotten that you are here to make a difference? I shake my head at the problems around me. I even take these concerns to God in prayer. But I know that because I am God's child, I am to do more than notice those who hurt. When I see injustice and judgment where only grace could possibly heal, I can be that giver of grace.

Ask God to change your dreams into his own. It's a big request, and many of us are afraid to state it for the record. What if we don't know how to right a wrong or heal a heart wound? What if our capacity to love the unlovable is too limited? What if this step disrupts the life to which we have grown accustomed? If these doubts expressed as questions hold you back from asking God to give you his dreams for your life, then ask God for his heart first. It is tender and willing and open. Ask God for his eyes. They see others clearly, they envision the big picture, and they witness the hurting world.

God does not tire of answering questions or of giving. But as he gives, he is waiting for your "yes." He wants to give you a dream that will transform your life.

Shedding Light:

- Will you replace your dream with God's dream for you?
- Seek ways to extend grace, to celebrate goodness, and to build up the hope in others.
- Be a healer and a dreamer. Live in God's truth, speak words of kindness, and reach out with actions of compassion.

Prayer:

I want to be a big dreamer who is willing to leap into a life so much bigger, deeper, greater, and more significant than I could ever imagine. This abundant life is the one you have mapped out for me. You direct my steps and you prompt my heart.

Afterglow:

I will carry the dreams of my Abba Father in my heart and into my tomorrow.

Counseling Session Two

*We must move from asking God to take care of
the things that are breaking our hearts, to praying
about the things that are breaking His heart.*

MARGARET GIBB

I think we got somewhere in the first session. Let's go back in for another. It seems like there is something else you'd like to address. Feel free.

> *Imaginary Counselor:* Anything from last session that was helpful?

> *You:* I know that I'm a human who makes mistakes and needs God.

> *IC:* Excellent. What's been happening?

> *You:* I feel lighter. God has transformed me and the former situation. It's too bad this awareness is trumped by a recent, unfortunate event.

> *IC:* What happened?

> *You:* Someone hurt me deeply. I can't get past it, and I don't think I ever will.

> *IC:* So you didn't give the situation or the person over to God?

> *You:* I tried, but that doesn't change how I feel about this person now.

> *IC:* God knows something that might help. I know it too. Ready?

You: Yes. Did I mention that I was deeply hurt and brokenhearted?

IC: Here it is. That person who hurt you is human. Just as you need to know that God is bigger than their sin and he loves them unconditionally—you *also* have to recognize and admit that other people are human. You can't fix this. God can.

You: That sounds familiar.

IC: The truths about God's love and forgiveness that transform your life are also available to others. Don't just pray for your life to go smoothly. Pray for that other person and their wholeness. But that will mean that you...

You: I know...I'll need God to do this, right?

IC: Absolutely.

Shedding Light:

- What have you been trying to fix on your own and in your own power? Ready, set, let go.

- The intimate, personal, transforming lessons of faith that you learn are also lessons about how God relates to others.

- Remember that the person you are struggling with is a person who is broken, just like you. Pray for their wholeness as well as your own.

Prayer:

God, I give you my heart and I give you my struggles with others. You know what is at stake in each relationship. You see where I am hardened. You watch me push buttons instead of embrace grace. Sometimes I think I hold onto my hurts because I don't want to admit my own transgressions. Transform this stubborn heart of mine, God.

Afterglow:

I'll apply what I learn about God's transforming power to my life and relationships with other fallible humans.

Light a Candle
for Grace

Taking Notes

In grief, one can endure the day, just the day. But when one also tries to bear the grief ahead, one cannot compass it. As for happiness, it can only be the ability to experience the moment. It is not next year that life will be so flawless and if we keep trying to wait for next year's happiness, the river of time will wind past and we shall not have lived at all.

GLADYS TABER, *STILLMEADOW DAY BOOK*

I mourn the fact that I've done very little journaling during the past couple of years. Many index cards bearing notes or quotes are crumpled in the bottom of my numerous purses and backpacks. But I feel the loss of not having a coherent gathering of my recollections because I've journeyed through a great trial and have learned about healing and mercy.

I imagine there are seasons when you are observing life, taking note of every drop of wisdom that comes to you, and sitting like a pupil eager to jot down God's truths as they are presented. You've probably also discovered, as I have, that there are seasons when we are called to invest every bit of ourselves into the living—when we cannot fully reflect on life as it is passing, or we will certainly miss being present for what God is teaching us. And do not be mistaken—these times of great work, grief, loss, perseverance, and endurance are teaching us about living and faithfulness.

I've missed having the time and distance to process my

faith journey. God has pulled me out of my comfort zone and into full, immediate, sometimes difficult, and always abundant living. The big lessons often emerge amidst a cyclone when there is no time to make sense of them during the experience. But if we are faithful and persevere in God's strength, those lessons are not lost in the uncertainty of a storm, for these God-lessons have been impressed upon our hearts to carry with us wherever the path leads.

Shedding Light:

- Is this a time to do more observing and reflecting? Or is it a time to press on in life...fully focused on the living? Maybe you are at that place of balance. No matter the season...stay connected to God and his voice.

- What certainty, learned during an earlier time of chaos or pain, do you carry today?

Prayer:

God, help me to understand the lessons I am to learn during this time. Help me to stand on the wonderful truths I've learned from my past trials. When the winds of change have rushed through my life, and I felt so out of control, you were the ever-present sense of peace. Carry me today as you did then. May I always praise you for your grace.

Afterglow:

I will allow eternal impressions to be made on my heart today, so that truth travels with me and changes me.

Landscape of Grace

*What would a sinless life look like? I can
only imagine. Strive as I may, I won't achieve
it. My interior landscape is scarred.*

CINDY CROSBY

Our eyes grow accustomed to the view from where we stand in life. The streets and intersections are known by heart. We can greet by name many of the people we encounter. Even the people we don't know have familiar faces, and we can nod to them. We know the best route to our favorite stores, and we slip into "our" spot at church, at work, and at our corner coffee shop. This view is consistent. Comfortable. And frankly it's one we could experience with our eyes closed.

We always need grace. But when we turn to its power with desperation and heart, our view tends to have shifted from the known to the unknown. We don't recognize the path, and there is little comfort found as we maneuver the unfamiliar. But there is grace. It opens our eyes to God's presence and his involvement with our lives. In times of sickness, healing rises. In seasons of despair, hope emerges. In days of fear, peace materializes. In moments of doubt, faith appears.

Be thankful to have your eyes opened to the landscape of

grace—it is as vast as the unknown. But in a life dependent on God, it becomes as familiar as the terrain of our own hearts.

Shedding Light:

- View the unfamiliar terrain as a good thing—an opportunity to shift from independence to total dependence on God.

- Change up your routine. You don't have to wait for a life change or trial to awaken to the landscape of grace. Step out more. Talk to new people. Take a risk by being vulnerable.

- Comfort is something to be grateful for. But getting too comfortable in life can undermine a sense of gratitude.

Prayer:

Open my eyes to what I am supposed to see. Open my eyes to what I am supposed to be. Open my eyes to see the ache in the person before me. Open my eyes to see the need in this culture of plenty. Open my eyes to witness healing in the middle of pain. Open my eyes to see the warm glow of grace cast against the shadow of my complacency.

Afterglow:

Today I'll resist the temptation to keep life predictable and experience the renewal of grace.

Falling Apart

*This thing that we call "failure" is not the
falling down, but the staying down.*

MARY PICKFORD

A huge bill arrives in the mail when you're financially tapped out. The kids are stuck in whine mode. You get one more serving of bad news than you can digest. Pressure at work and at home makes it impossible to pretend everything is fine. Or maybe you have one day filled with a series of misfortunate events that leaves you floored and unsure how to get back up.

Why is it that "pick yourself up and dust yourself off" sounds like encouragement when we're saying it to a five-year-old, but when we say it to ourselves, it sounds unfeeling, even cruel? First of all you aren't hurting because someone is in your favorite swing. Second "pick yourself up" outlives its effectiveness after about 20 times. But having faith means you have more than clichés for consolation—you have God's comfort and strength to get you back on your feet.

A friend and I contemplated what life would be like if we rarely experienced "failure" or circumstances that knocked us over. We wouldn't rely on God's mercy and power. We wouldn't know the wonder of grace or gratitude. And we wouldn't have the sweet assurance that when life is hard, we haven't fallen from grace—we're being carried by it.

Shedding Light:

- What does grace mean to you? How does God's grace impact your life and how you view your trials?

- Have you told yourself to "pick yourself up" so many times that it feels unkind? Be gentle with yourself when you struggle. Go to God. He'll give you strength along with kind, helpful words.

Prayer:

God, lift me up out of this circumstance. I feel tired and useless. I'm such a pro at grinning and bearing it that I've forgotten how to process my emotions when something does go wrong. I want to feel the struggle only so that I can bring it to you honestly. I won't hide bits of it from myself or you so that I appear stronger. I want to lean into your strength and be carried by grace.

Afterglow:

Tough days are nothing new. But how I treat them and myself during the tough days will be a new thing.

A New Direction

*I do not at all understand the mystery of
grace—only that it meets us where we are
but does not leave us where it found us.*

ANNE LAMOTT

I saw a young boy pacing in front of a driveway while he
waited impatiently for his parents to finish talking with
friends. The last time I saw pacing was in a 1950's comedy
where the husband robotically walked the width of a
maternity ward hallway. The thing about walking back and
forth is that you don't get anywhere, no matter how many
times you do it (just ask the boy).

When we are pacing, trying to find our way out of a box
created by sin, frailty, pride, lack of wisdom, or any number
of things, it is only God and his grace that can get us out of
this futile pattern. His grace covers us and transforms us. It
does not leave us to walk into a wall, turn around, and start
all over again…it leads us beyond the limits of our sin and
humanity and allows us to walk in God's freedom.

When we are going nowhere, God's grace changes
that. He does not leave us where he finds us. He gives us
a new direction and the hope of healing, and he sets us in
motion…going forward toward a future.

Shedding Light:

- What is making you pace right now? Are you getting weary from this pattern of going nowhere? Go to God and ask for a new path through familiar troubles.

- Sins and lies and unhealthy relationships box us in. And when we try to correct these, on our own with human solutions, we're usually just building a slightly bigger box around the old one.

- Walking in God's freedom will feel different. You'll discover a life without limits.

Prayer:

God, I walk back and forth carrying my broken pieces. I show them to others and we take notes about the brokenness. I add pieces to the pile because I tell myself there's no time to place them in your hands. No wonder I'm overwhelmed... I'm saving and transporting the very pieces you have asked me to surrender. I'm ready to give these up. I might not like it at first. What will I do when I don't have to tend to my brokenness day in and day out?

Afterglow:

I plan to discover what it feels like to be unburdened. I plan to live in grace.

A Brave Grace

Courage is fear that has said its prayers.

DOROTHY BERNARD

Life requires courageous steps, big and small. Sometimes just getting out of bed is an act of bravery. Following God's leading when it is outside of our expectations or plans is an act of courage. Trusting God's forgiveness when we feel unworthy is an act of courage. And that kind of courage is ours only when we depend on God through and in spite of our fears. Such strength becomes a part of our character when we face a conflict, a need, or an average day head-on with prayer. When we can look at our lives as an offering, a sacrifice to God, then we are acting with fierce faith.

"Saying grace" seems an old-fashioned term for prayer. Rarely do you hear this particular phrase mentioned at a dining table where pizza is served and those gathering around are 15 minutes late to soccer practice or eager to get back to their computer games. But saying grace is a way to introduce our side of grace—giving thanks. Bring the act of giving thanks back into your life and the lives of your family members. It will lead them to greater faith. It will lead them to gratitude. It will lead them to courage.

Shedding Light:

- Why do you feel unworthy? Sometimes the thing or the person or the event that initially caused us to feel unworthy is not even something in our present life. We've just been afraid to believe in something better.

- How are you strong? In what ways do you exhibit strength and truth in your life?

- Spend time giving thanks for your recent joys, the latest problems, and those past happenings that gave root to bitterness. These all are meant to lead you to God. What could give us more gratitude than that?

Prayer:

I've spent a lot of time dwelling on my fears. Even though I know you and your peace, I turn back to the way of fear. Lead me through these times. When simple worries morph into a foundation of fear, I will return to the courage I have in you. I need not tremble. I need not avoid living. Thank you for every circumstance that turns my thoughts back to you and my heart toward you.

Afterglow:

I'll embrace courage as a God-given character trait, and I will give thanks!

Light a Candle
for Sanctuary

Shaping Space for God

As I started looking, I found more and more.

VALERIE STEELE

In a magazine interview, singer Dolly Parton mentioned that, on all of her properties, she has either a chapel or an area with a *prie dieu* kneeler, so that she can take time for prayer and silence during a busy life. I loved this idea, and it reminded me of some of my past goals related to making room for God and prayer. For some time I have wanted to create a space in my home for this very thing, but I have put it off. For some time I have wanted to discipline myself to read and reflect on Scripture and journal my responses to it, but I have put it off.

When life throws obstacles in our way or troubles arise, we do not hesitate to seek God immediately. We ask for a meeting right then and there. Wouldn't it be so much better if we had an ongoing session scheduled with God all ready? Wouldn't it be great if we gave our hearts and minds and lives over to God daily and felt that immediate sense of his presence no matter what our circumstances?

Don't put off making space for God in your life. Set aside a very deliberate, special, meaningful portion of your day, your heart, and your home and dedicate them to God.

The more you seek God throughout your day, the more intimately you'll know God.

Shedding Light:

- Prepare a place of prayer in your life. Make this a meaningful space. Maybe that comfy chair that only gets used when company comes over can be placed near a window for your special spot. Maybe your sanctuary is a walking path along a river. You don't have to sit to meditate and pray.

- Go back to the tried and true Sunday school practice of memorizing verses. Rest in the comfort, inspiration, and peace they offer…that God offers.

Prayer:

Give me a heart that seeks the refuge of your love automatically. Whether I'm making decisions, facing sickness or struggle, or walking an unplanned course…I will start my journey in your sanctuary. I will praise you as I enter your presence, and I will listen for your leading.

Afterglow:

I will connect with God more frequently, so that the path to his presence becomes familiar to my heart and soul.

An Unfolding Mystery

In all that I value, there is a core of mystery.

MARGE PIERCY

There is mystery tied to faith. That can scare some. It can intimidate others. But if you consider for one moment how incredibly refreshing it is to not know all the answers, you'll understand the allure of deep faith. In an age when we can look up a definition, a history, a ten-year plan for almost anything and everything via the internet, we should embrace the idea of faith. Faith influences our lives. It defines us. It leads us through days that would, without faith, make us drop to our knees in defeat.

As much as we study, research, pick apart, and analyze faith, it still beholds the beauty of mystery. This is such a lovely part of belief, and yet we want to feel "in the know" and in control of the information that relates to what we base our life on. That is understandable, but our desire for absolutes undermines the wonder of miracles, and it steals the joy that could be ours for holding onto belief even when we *don't* know all the answers.

Celebrate the unknowns of faith. If we could pinpoint every single truth of faith, it might make us sought-out scholars, but it would do little to build up our hope in the Lord. The world holds such little potential for mystery and wonder. We are the privileged few—those of us who cling to hope not only in spite of the questions but because of them.

Shedding Light:

- Have you ever thought about how freeing it is to *not* know all the answers? Spend time praying about this newly recognized freedom. How might your daily life change once you rest in this freedom?

- When you share faith with others, take time to step away from theology and debate and describe the intimate beauty of faith that you have personally experienced.

Prayer:

Lead me to wonder. When I try to define you and your love, let me rest with the same assurance in the aspects of you and your nature that I can and cannot define. Thank you for delighting me with surprises that take my breath away and reminding me of the miracle of life and the wonders of how you work in and through circumstances and people.

Afterglow:

I will live as a person who believes in miracles and who honors the mystery of faith.

Passport

Send out your light and your truth; let them guide me.

PSALM 43:3

What transports you to a sanctuary mind-set? The travel friend I mentioned in my intro was feeling a strong pull to return to Europe. I had been craving the same. Since her life was incredibly busy and a quick jaunt to another country was hardly feasible, she decided to go to a local coffeehouse, order a cappuccino in a mug, and sit at a table for a few minutes. Not quite a Parisian vacation, and yet it was her passport to happiness. A couple weeks later, she and I enjoyed several cappuccinos together in similar fashion. It led us both back to the fun and camaraderie of our original trip. I was grateful for the opportunity.

Is there a time or place you think of that fills you with joy? Is there a way for you to recapture that same feeling? I find that when I look at photos of a happy moment in my life or of someone that I care about, I smile, relax, and settle into contentment. When I revisit a favorite book during a rare, leisurely afternoon, I am refreshed and satisfied. We forget to take time for important moments of peace, reflection, and joy.

If you've struggled to create a practice of daily meditation and devotion, find ways to recapture the joy of spending time with God. A few moments in prayer will transport you to God's presence. You'll be grateful for the opportunity.

Shedding Light:

- When was the last time you experienced pure joy? Can you duplicate this or recreate it in a new form today?
- Prayer can be a passport out of regret and into the land of peace. It can transport you from a time of self-focus to a place of compassion. Prayer changes your heart and where you stand in faith.

Prayer:

Take me away from the monotony of today. I barely can distinguish today from yesterday or the week before. I want to savor these moments of family, interaction, new challenges, and living. God, help me watch for the joy that can grace even the most routine day. Lead me to people who readily share joy and direct my spirit and mind-set to receive happiness like manna from heaven.

Afterglow:

I will retrace my steps to a place of happiness. God is there, and he'll help me bring forth the joy in my life.

Spiritual Garden Sanctuary

*The greatest gift of the garden is the
restoration of the five senses.*

HANNA RION

Having a sanctuary to go to is a gift. There is a hilltop garden in our town. When spring comes around each year, this is a tranquil place to wander along pea gravel paths under a canopy of vibrantly colored flowers and shade-giving foliage. Many caring hands and hearts have worked to create such a sacred space, and I am blessed to reap the benefits. At the crest of the hill is a lookout. From here the busyness of life fades to the background and the beauty of life comes to the forefront.

A heart that is given over to God becomes a sanctuary that, no matter the season, provides a tranquil refuge. Such a sacred space can be created when we allow moments of stillness to become intentional sessions of prayer and reflection, not fleeting intermissions. When we evaluate our lives and weed out the chaos so that peace and meaning can grow, we are tending to this inner garden. And when we choose to walk alongside God rather than rush past him with our own agendas and routes, we will see the sights he intends for us to experience.

Take time to revel in reverence and awe of God's

goodness here in the spiritual sanctuary of your heart. Here the busyness of life fades to the background, and the beauty of life comes to the forefront…and you are richly blessed as your senses awaken.

Shedding Light:

- Quiet is not absence. Stillness is not inaction. Sanctuary is not escape.
- Invite God's goodness to infuse your existence. Only then can you know it intimately. Only then can you share it.
- Even if you don't run around with your every move planned, chances are you live by your own agenda. Try to give that over to God this week. Leave space for what God might be offering you. It might be rest, a conversation, an idea, a prayer. God only knows!

Prayer:

I don't always see the weeds that crop up in my habits and plans. God, point out those activities, thoughts, and expectations that don't belong in the sanctuary you've planned for me. Give me the discipline and discernment to rid my life of them. I want to make room for the flowers of hope and potential you plant alongside my journey's road.

Afterglow:

I am a blessed child of God. I'll walk forward in this identity rather than one shaped by my success, performance, or goals.

So Good

Taste and see that the LORD is good. Oh, the
joys of those who take refuge in him!

PSALM 34:8

I t's so good to be here, in this place of refuge. This is the
heart of God. Some might mistakenly see God's refuge
as a barrier that separates us from the world. They might
want it to become a protective wall between our hearts
and the harsh times of doubt. But those scenarios aren't
examples of godly refuge, they're illustrations of separation
and confinement.

God's refuge is a garden with plenty of benches on which
to sit and think and pray. God's refuge is an open field where
we can walk for miles safely and happily, even when storm
clouds rumble above. God's refuge is a gentle valley where
we can climb to the top of a hill at night and watch the stars
with pure joy and wonder.

I don't think God's refuge has a lot of posted rules. I think
that when we are here in it, when our hearts are longing
for communion with God, we are gently nudged in the
right directions and lovingly taught the things of goodness
and meaning. We see paths with greater understanding,
discernment, and clarity. And we see the needs and hearts of
others with less judgment and more compassion.

How do you know when you are in God's presence? By the heightened awareness of what is good and life-giving.

Shedding Light:

- Did you grow up with a lot of rules and very little gentle guidance? It can be difficult to discern the voice of God when we have not known the voice of love in our human relationships. Consider studying the ways of God's love during your time of meditation.

- Has there been a time when you used the idea of refuge to close yourself off from the world? If you are still there, find a way beyond this self-prescribed gated community. Start living a life of faith out where it can have influence and effect.

Prayer:

I'll run and run and never reach the limits of your love. I'll stare at the sky throughout the night and never see its edges. There is comfort in the limitless expanse of your love and compassion. Teach me to breathe deeply and rest in this freedom. May I recognize that which is pure and noble and good in this life.

Afterglow:

With the goal of freedom, I will tear down this protective wall that I built or that others built for me.

The Way of the Heart

I wonder sometimes if we haven't banished the way of the heart in favor of the way of the mind, if we emphasize learning about God over being with God.

SUE MONK KIDD, *WHEN THE HEART WAITS*

Light a candle. Watch the flame. Don't force yourself into thoughts or pressure yourself to come up with the right words to say. When your heart wants to create an offering of a simple prayer, your mind mentions that God created Kilimanjaro and gravity and all of a sudden…those words about hope and thanksgiving seem meager and insignificant. When your heart is ready to share its brokenness, your mind weighs the labor involved in healing and wholeness, and you second-guess embarking on the journey. How often do we get in our own way of sweet communion with God?

But when you enter God's presence, you'll feel comforted rather than burdened by the mystery of the unknown. You'll be able to let go of the loud inner-judge and give way to God's grace and acceptance. But you have to leave the way of the world, the way of control and preconceived notions, at the door of your sanctuary, whether it is a church, a room, or your heart.

Just for once (or even better, try it as a regular habit) let go of your head knowledge of prayer and God. That knowledge is important, and useful, and builds your foundation to faith...but right now, in this moment, let your heart take over. It has amazing things to share with its Creator. And it will lead you to sanctuary.

Shedding Light:

- Let your heart speak. What does it want to say to God? What has prevented you from allowing your heart to speak honestly in the past?
- When you are with God...be with him fully, wholly, and with an open heart and spirit.

Prayer:

God, my heart is ready to express its love, its hurts, and its longings. My mind is ready to quit overriding what my heart wants to share and receive. I'm made to have intimacy with you. Thank you for preparing in me that desire for communication and for the peace that comes only from your heart. The gift of sanctuary permeates my life. All I want is to be with you.

Afterglow:

I will make prayer a priority. I will follow the way of the heart straight to God's presence.

About the Author

Hope Lyda has worked in publishing for twelve years and is the author of several novels including *Life, Libby, and the Pursuit of Happiness* in addition to numerous nonfiction titles such as the popular One-Minute Prayers series (more than 520,000 copies sold). When Hope isn't helping others in their writing endeavors as an editor, she can be found working on her latest writing project while at a local coffee shop or jotting down ideas on 3 x 5 cards or any piece of scrap paper that's handy. She and her husband live in Oregon where they enjoy the relaxed lifestyle and beauty of the Northwest and the opportunity to head to the coast in a moment's notice.

You can email Hope at
hopelyda@yahoo.com

Other inspirational books
by Hope Lyda

〰

One Minute with God

One Minute with God for Women

Prayers of Comfort for Those Who Hurt

One-Minute Prayers™

One-Minute Prayers™ for Healing

One-Minute Prayers™ for Women

One-Minute Prayers™ for Wives

One-Minute Prayers™ to Start Your Day

One-Minute Prayers™ to End Your Day